ORDER OUT OF CHAOS

By

EM KHEI

Contents

INTRODUCTION

We are currently living in an ocean of chaos from every aspect in the present world. By saying chaos I don't however imply that we have fights among ourselves, though the absence of wars doesn't necessarily mean that there is individual peace.

Every area of human existence is chaotic and in disorder though not consciously noticed by man. We are always on the run and rush to perfect our lives, seeking something which in most cases is never found. Sometimes life can be confusing in that nothing satisfies man no matter what he has achieved in his personal life.

This book will revolve around the human life and point out some areas, mentalities, perceptions and the like, which has resulted to the present world confusion and chaotic experience. This book will also point out what needs to be changed or transcended, in order for that which is Planned to bring order to be effective and beneficial to man.

Everyone is aware that there are Powers which are behind life; Those Who feed Life to what is considered life by man. Please note that I'm not talking of a god or satan/devil here, though the name doesn't matter in this material.

Life can be confusing at times and one may wonder why we face all that we experience in our lifetimes, but what if existence wasn't shaped in the manner we perceive it? What if we don't live as per the Design of the **Great Ones**? What if our lives were supposed to be perfect and orderly, but we are the ones who have turned it chaotic and disorderly?

Some questions have no specific answers and so is to life and existence where there is no specific way to live.

This book will outline some of our behaviors, monotonies and the like which have resulted to the present chaos and also some Revelations into The New Day where Order will be eminent. I therefore welcome you to a subject less discussed and to things which are feared by the masses about life and existence. I would like to give a disclaimer to my readers that let no one approach any of my works with their perceived truths and perceptions since I will definitely disappoint; I know I can be very good in that.

I have no personal affiliation to any religious beliefs or cultural perceptions and so everything I share will be contradicting to the norms and perceptions of the masses. It's therefore advisable to anyone reading any of my materials to approach them with an open mind and a readiness to real life application for comprehension or for the material to make sense.

Many things which I will share will also contain some encoded messages which will require individual effort to decode and so let not everything be understood in the manner it lamely appears to mean. Many discoveries will be found in the many hidden meanings of phrases, words and statements incorporated in my writings.

I don't want to however give an impression that I know everything or the material contains the Universal truths, but maybe it can lead to their discovery. Much of my works revolve around the New Ways of Life which The New Day carries, and which require individual partaking and application for the benefit of human future and the world as a whole.

Don't forget to take your time and research (if anything related to what I write will have a reference), and try to look at life in a different angle. I'm however aware that many things will not make sense at the time, but as time unfolds, many will start to see the reality as it truly is.

Remember that much of what my writings contain has no reference and someone might even spend the rest of their lives trying to find where they are derived from and die having never found anything that relates to my materials. But don't assume I'm a prophet or something of the sort, I'm just a simple man like any other but just because whatever I share have no reference doesn't mean that it's a lie or made-up story.

The most valuable thing is the hardest to find.

- Manly P. Hall

THE HUMAN MIND

The mind is a very powerful tool in a human being, and it's often the creator and the destroyer of reality, perceptions and the like. The mind is the discriminator of what an individual considers important and that which he considers less important, which brings about the present world chaos between the perceived right and wrong.

You'll have to agree with me that what you consider right is not always right to everyone, and what you consider wrong or evil is not always the case to everyone. People are very quick to label things without understanding that what they value is not always valuable to everyone.

Through the individual discrimination of things, everyone assumes that what they label as important is always important to everyone, forgetting that assumption is a deadly friend. Although everyone has got their individual minds, it doesn't mean that every mind operates the same way as everyone else's. This' a fact that is often overlooked, with the perception that because you think that something should be in a certain way, or people should behave in a certain way (just because you do, or those around you do), you assume that it's the "right/correct" way to do things or live.

Through this, certain qualities start to emerge, where division comes in. Someone starts to identify with a certain perception, belief, group and the like, considering the others who are not relating to their perceptions as wrong or even evil. Through this discrimination of the mind and identifying with certain things which appear "right" or "correct" to us, we start hating those who are "different" from us; whether by belief, styles of living and doing things, and even color, race and the like.

This leads to division among people and identities are born, just like the perception of good and bad is born in the minds of men. For your information, there is nothing like good, bad, evil, right, wrong, and all the related dual creations of the human mind. They are just born from the limited discrimination of the human mind, basing it on the interests of the individual which are only confined in form.

Today the world is divided, full of hate and the like due to this discriminating force of the mind, resulting to the present identities where everyone seeks to identify themselves with the groups, beliefs, colors, races, and the like, which only support their points of view as per their mind's discrimination and identity.

We have everything we need, but we barely know about it. Humans are only concerned with the physical, forgetting that there is the unseen world which operates also in the physical world and extends "outwards."

We only concentrate on the form and that's where the problem comes in. When you look at the other person, your concern is only on the outer expression, forgetting that the form is just a vehicle in which the soul expresses itself through. Like I mentioned in another material (which will be released later for specific reasons), the human mind is cocooned in form due to the concentration and conditioning of the human being in the material reality and that's why the brain cannot exist without the mind, though the mind can exist without the brain.

The human mind is always handicapped by the concentration of man on the form only, which closes the door to Universality of Beingness, keeping him off from the Universal Mind which identifies not with the part (as the human mind through discrimination), but with the whole (since there is only One Life).

Through this identification with the part, we see the present world which is divided on groups, whether religious, political, racial, geographical location, and the like, where each wants to be a part of what his mind identifies with and in which his mind favors as good or right. Many will not believe or agree with me, but it's the mind which has resulted to the major rift between human beings.

If I identify with the white, the black will always be evil to me; if I identify with the black, the white will always be my enemy. These limited and divisive mentalities and perceptions rule the present world where even when an employer seeks employees, many discriminate who to employ and who not to basing it on these identities other than qualifications. I've seen people of the same color discriminating each other on tribal lines, I've seen people discriminating each other on the line of color, and I've seen people discriminate each other on the line of beliefs (whether cultural or religious). The list is endless.

Everywhere in the world at any level, whether governments who serve same people, to religious beliefs which claim to serve all, this division is explicit. We are divided; our minds are always at war with each other's point of view, color, race, geographical location, and all the human identities that exist. Everyone is ready to fight his brother, just because he doesn't follow or fall under their identities and perceptions.

We might not be at physical wars with each other, but we always fight each other. It's through the mind's ability to discriminate on the line of the "Lower Aspects of life" that are only confined in form that we witness the today's world full of chaos based on limited identities and mentalities.

A person will hate his brother due to his color; another will hate his brother due to what he believes in, another will hate his brother because he doesn't come from his cultural background or difference in language. The list is inexhaustible. Just look around and see the division that exists between us. I also know that many will hate me after they've read certain materials which will be released after this because they contain some information which will be scary and which many will consider evil and start labeling me in the lines of their individual perceptions and through fear of their contents.

Many will give me names and identities after they've read those materials because they challenge the norms and go against the modern societies, lifestyles and perceptions.

Man should understand that what they identify with is of less importance, what you believe in isn't important, your color is just an illusory difference and label which is only confined in form and on the lower aspect of existence. Your identities are meaningless and will help no man, rather, they will only divide and cause unnecessary chaos and perceptions which will only eat man bit-by-bit until he wakes up to the reality of life and existence (if he really wakes up).

All must understand that form is just a vehicle of expression designed not as understood and used by man, but to serve the Spirit. People must shun identifying with form and limited perceptions which are there to destroy humanity rather than make him grow and serve the Plan. Don't lie to yourself that whatever you see is a part of the true reality. Yes it's in the reality of the human mind held tight by the perceived "common senses," but beyond the physical, all is just fantasy and illusions.

Identities will take us nowhere. They will not save man from what lies ahead, but rather they will destroy him. Whatever you identify with will not help you in the hour of need and in the darkest night which is at the horizons. Man has to learn to identify himself not with the part, but with the whole of humanity regardless of color, belief, language, geographical boundaries, and the like.

We must learn to live together as brothers, or perish together as fools.

-Martin Luther King Jr.

The world needs LOVE the most (and when I say love I would like to emphasize like I always do in almost each of my writings that I don't mean the perceived love), at the moment. What is on the way doesn't care about who one considers themselves as, or what group they identify with since none of that matter.

Out of many, One. (There is a deeper esoteric meaning of the phrase which is outside the scope of this material and so will not be discussed here).

We are One; Life is One, though expressing itself in many forms. No one is important than the other, no belief system (religious or cultural), is more valuable than the other. Nothing is good, and nothing is bad since those are just human creations of the mind. All are equal, though divided and separated by illusory identities and perceptions. All must work together, unite and seek that which is beyond form. You'll discover that that is not a request or an option very soon worldwide. Revelation about that will be released later after this material.

Humans have to learn to live as souls. Being in the world but not of it; Living not for the form and its confines, but rather to live for the Higher Aspects/Ideals of existence. For unity and right human relation in the world, all must transcend their individual minds. He, who transcends his mind gets the release from limited identities, beliefs, perceptions and the like and lives as per the Great Design.

It's the identities created by the mind that has brought about the present world crisis and division among men. Everyone fights what they don't understand, seeks to identify with certain beliefs, perceptions and the like for safety, leading to the present world separation and hate which is feeding on humanity slowly. Love is the key; identities will only lead to chaos. Balance/harmony will only be achieved in the world if man will learn to shun his little identities and labels, and understand that he's just a minute thing in creation; a part of the whole which is always dependent on each other to produce the Universal Beauty that exists and that which The Great Ones seek to see in the world.

RELIGIOUS FAITH AND BELIEFS

Many of my materials have touched this subject, which means that the world is waited by a "rude awakening" regarding the belief systems. (Don't ask yourself why this material comes first before the materials which were written before it; there is a reason for that). This subject has carried much of the human problems in the world due to its "lower application" and dogmas associated with it which have turned many to fanatics.

Beliefs have played a very big role in dividing man among himself and results to the hate that we have in the world in relation to beliefs (religious and cultural). Whatever belief system one identifies himself with won't matter and will never matter since as of now, they have proven useless and poison to the human existence and their time is nearing the end.

People are very quick to show everyone how they are believers of a certain faith; they will pretend to be so knowledgeable about how humans are expected to live as per their religious books of reference, but sadly they don't even live those teachings. Better a non-believer, who lives the way they feel they should without pretending to be holly in the eyes of men, than a hypocrite who tries to convince everyone how good they are but their lives are just a lie.

When it comes to the issue of religion and beliefs, I oftentimes get unapologetic on what I say and don't care about who one considers themselves to be since that doesn't matter not only to me, but even to The Great Ones.

Facing life with truth will give man freedom, but facing it with hypocrisy will destroy him.

We consider ourselves believers but we don't live the belief itself. I've seen religious people plot evil and even murders of their brothers. I've seen people who claim to be the "shepherds of the flock" take advantage of the flock they claim to be guiding. Everywhere in the world we see these people who live two different lives; the life they want everyone to think they live, and the life they live in the dark.

"Destruction" of humanity is inevitable due to ignorance. You'll discover that in a different material. Life is free, but can be very costly when lived ignorantly. No mercy.

We claim to be equal and even preach it to our brothers, but we have hate engraved in our hearts. It's like a person sharing a smile with you, but behind his back he holds tight a dagger to stab you. That's the world of today. We live lies, lying to others as well as ourselves. A person will be the epicenter of his congregation, but at night he sleeps with the wives of his followers. These things are among us and happen every day.

Religion is thought (by the fanatics) as the route to human liberation, with these people thinking that they can live the way they think as right, just because they have the illusory "promised land" elsewhere. Through this, they can live the way they wish, even destroying the very world they reside in, with the perception of "live life to the fullest since you only live once" because to them, their god/allah/jehovah/satan/devil, or whatever they may call the character, is merciful and will redeem them in the end.

I'm not here to talk about The Powers that Control the World because very soon humanity will face reality as it is (and it won't be a sweet experience), but my point is that we approach life with ignorance forgetting that The Great Ones are ruthless to ignorance and radical changes are underway to shape the New World that "WE" are aiding its foundation.

Don't forget that all these ignorant behaviors and mentalities lead to a chaotic experience which to some degree is catastrophic. Beliefs are not the route to order or world peace and unity, they have proven themselves as only tools to fanaticism which is destructive, to individuals and to the world at large.

Seek individual connection with the Deity, seek to live not as you think it's the right way to live, but in a way you are certain that you are living a genuine life free of ignorance. Seek the divinity within and live as per its guide and you'll discover that you'll even feel free from the constraints of limited beliefs which are just divisive.

Each person is their individual saviors. Whatever you think you know as truth now will matter less in near future where there will be no dogmatic beliefs and fanaticism guided by ignorance. Live responsibly, being aware that everything has a price and in the end each must be paid; whether individually or globally.

The plan must work out and things go as they should. You might be free to live the way you want, following ways which you feel to be right to you, but when ignorance takes over, consequences are eminent. The world needs a new universal belief system which doesn't divide on lines of language, color, race, and the like, but that which unites all to the universality of existence and love divine which seeks harmony in all areas of human existence.

Remember, the Universe can only be discovered by direct experience alone, not through the "avenues" followed by man.

LIFTING OF THE CURTAINS

Time is running out and as I stated in a different material, there is the urgent need of the catalyst to speed up "things" so as to produce the desired beauty and to work out the Plan. Many will not agree with me that most of what we value as human beings is just useless and all we think we know as truth in the world today is just but lies which have been implanted in our brains and made to seem like truth.

But luckily much has been allowed to be released to the human race so far and much more is on the way when the time is right. We live fantasy lives which are guided and controlled by illusions and lies, but we are made to believe them as the true reality or truth.

At the moment there is so much still hidden from man because he is still rooted in his fantasies that he cannot realize his blindness. It's very interesting to find out that we live lies, believe lies and follow lies as norms confined in existence. For example humans believe that life is all about what happens around us, or what we just see. It's however unfortunate that even those who realize that there is an intertwined reality within our own reality which we can't see or recognize (since we are generally blocked from seeing it because we are not yet ready for that reality), create another illusion with the religious perceptions which are but control mechanisms.

Please note that there is the presence of The Prime One who operates with the help of The Great Ones (The Lord of the World – not earth - and The Hierarchy included). Many will try to convince themselves that this Prime One is just the other name for their god or satan/devil or whatever name they call their religious characters, but don't lie to yourself like that. The constituents of the Powers that Control the world is very intricate that one can only get confused while trying to understand it.

Like I've pointed out in other previous materials, everything religion teaches is nothing but lies and fear to keep its followers on their knees. Religion is a cleverly designed control machine with believers being turned into slaves to their own existence. Whether you believe in a god, devil, satan, allah, jesus, mohammed, and all the religious characters that are there globally, just be aware that those are just manufactured characters to keep you shut from the true Divinity and from connecting with The Custodians of Life so that you will never get access to your own powers and capabilities and know the truth.

I should also like to point out that there is the presence of a Cosmic Christ (not in relation to religious beliefs), but not jesus; Note the difference since many might be confused. The Hierarchy operates through the Christ Principle (not as perceived by the religious beliefs),since it's the closest "level" – The Hierarchy - (not in relation to superiority or such) to humanity since the Christ Principle is prime in this solar system. I've clarified that since I've not touched it in the previous materials when talking about the subject of religion and beliefs.

The time is upon us when the truth about these subjects will be revealed to the very eyes of men and they will discover the lies they have been living in, following beliefs and monotonies considered as "normal" while in reality they will never help them in their hour of need that is at the horizons.

Sometimes people don't believe in theories, and so will require practicality of things to accept them as truth, and so very soon (though it started a while back, and proceeding gradually), humans will experience a rude awakening where everything that made sense to them will become useless.

There is a "New Wave" sweeping the world that will leave nothing standing. The problem is that humans only perceive things the way that it suits them or in the way that it favors their individual fantasies to a point where even something which was meant to be applied in the higher aspect is often mistaken and misapplied, due to the lower aspects that guide the human existence.

For example there are those people who have turned to spirituality due to their search of freedom and connecting with their divinity within since they have noted something not right regarding religious beliefs. However, this spirituality has turned to be another illusory belief system which is only concerned with the form nature of man and hypocrisy in its operations. Spirituality and religion are just similar things which are just guided by illusions and misled ideologies which instead of helping human beings, it's acting as the blocking agent to the discovery of truth. Neither religion nor spirituality will give man freedom or awakening, but will rather just hold him captive in fantasies and illusions; they are both lower natures which just serve the limited beliefs and mentalities of man.

Whether you are a spiritual person or religious, whatever you think you believe is just similar, only approached in a different way from each other. Spirituality and religion are just created in the same ideology of lies and illusions. Whatever you claim to be standing for is just individual fantasies which will lead you nowhere.

These two belief systems will soon experience their demise and they will be replaced by that which will bring order and serve the common good of all. They have turned their followers into fanatics who just concentrate on form, thinking that it's of great value than Life itself. The believers and followers of these groups are very good at being concerned with what happens around themselves, but that which is inside of them is not serving which they claim to stand for.

It's for example through spirituality that we have the new age fanaticism worldwide. There is a new age, I don't deny that, and I've even written much of my materials revolving around it and mentioning it, but what people don't realize is the radical changes that will be experienced which will even cost the lives of millions due to the human ignorance.

There is the other cultural beliefs that are coming up (or being revived in different parts of the world – my part of world being one), which are playing the same fanatical roles. What will happen is that as religion gets overtaken by spirituality, then cultural beliefs appear to gain strength, (there is no order in their happenstance since that will depend on the part of the world that is concerned), all will later be treaded upon and as the New Civilization emerges and starts to take over, new "belief systems" (not necessarily beliefs as it sounds but individual illumination and awakening to the truth and reality) will emerge and the Universal Balance which "WE" are paving way for will be established.

14

No belief system will help man to wake up to the realization of the divinity, but individual efforts and being honest in your own way of life. Everything else will only mislead and keep you "low" since it's designed to keep you captive and a slave to your own existence.

Man will experience things which will lead him to the awakening to the lies he has been living in while thinking that he is living right. After everything is brought to his realization, he will discover that whatever he thinks as truth is nowhere even close to the truth. Many will try to seek a savior without success, try to scream loud but no one will be hearing their cries. We are nearing to the convergence of two realities to bring about the desired harmony; but as you are aware, whenever two waves meet, there is always the initial chaos and destruction which is later followed by calmness.

The meaning of existence will be understood and truth revealed. The illusions which have been a part of the human existence will vanish and man will find himself naked in the "garden of Eden" alone, with no one to turn to. Note that truth is the prime value an individual can acquire, but before that is possible, the largest global crisis will be unavoidable. Like I said in a different material, we have seen nothing yet since we are yet to the darkest part of the night that is at the horizons, and so before The New Day emerges, we have to face darkness and before we can have order, chaos will be experienced. I'm not a prophet or anything related (never forget that), but those are approved occurrences which await humanity.

HUMAN GOVERNANCE

All over the world we have the political regions (nations), which are run individually by a few people considered to be leaders (of which not all are). Each nation has its own set rules and rulers who decide on the way of life of their fellow citizens.

Since dawn of time, we have been having people in power and others who have been ruled. We have witnessed the differences emerge among nations or people in power where consequences hit hard those ruled. Wars have emerged between nations and even world wars which have divided the world into regions basing it on which ideologies each region supports. Through this we experience division on interests, whether by nations or politicians themselves individually.

At the present times, we cannot yet say that we have matured from these things. We still witness division on interests, ideologies and the like. Man has not yet learnt from his past, and he doesn't even seem concerned about it. He still concentrates on dominating or conquering those he assumes inferior from him (whether individuals or nations). Nations still plot evil even to their own citizens just to make a point or if those in power want to pass a certain law or bring in a certain ideology.

We cannot run from truth as it is at this time. These things happen; we see them being planned and executed by the same people who later come in to offer solutions. At these interesting times, the doctor is the creator of the disease he offers to treat his patients. The problem with the world today is that humans don't believe theories, and so they have to be made experience so as to believe.

Our present governments have to some degree disappointed us. They are not playing the role they are supposed to be playing. Those running them are just politicians who are just all about politicking; very few are leaders. Instead of serving their people they are dividing, with those in power oppressing those they rule, making petty laws which keep the poor poorer, while keeping power to a few.

A time is coming when enough will be enough and the masses will seek their rights and true representation by these governments and politicians. We have started to see this, and if nothing is done, the world is faced by a global crisis of people in the streets seeking equality on representation, allocation of resources and the like.

The governments must represent all (not a request). BALANCE must be established in the world and equality attained. No one is above anyone; being a political leader doesn't make one consequence-free. There is a new global wave coming which will crumble even the strongest of the governments. For the world to be a better place, governments must work for the good of all and stop petty politicking and instead work for the common good.

The world needs leaders, not politicians. We have the present world problem since we are ruled by politicians, not leaders and that's why governments have always been focusing on petty laws and policies which are just after enslaving the masses, corruption and misuse of resources for the benefit of a few while those who elect these people remain poor and struggling.

The playground will soon be leveled and harmony be established globally, with the focus being for the common good, rather than the political interests of a few. Sometimes one has to fall, to recognize the value and responsibilities associated with the rise, and so will governments and their officials. In the end of the crisis, what is intended will be established and peace, love and harmony will guide the new world.

Those who are true leaders, those who are after the betterment of all, free of personal interests, will lead the others. The world will establish unity and petty officials and laws will be done away with. The world does not need politicians, but leaders. The world doesn't need useless laws which are just after the benefit of some; oppressing the masses, while those assuming to be above others oppressing their people and selfishly siphoning the available resources to themselves.

Change is at the horizons. No one is prime or an exception to the intended world change. The plan will be worked out as designed and nothing or no one will stop or interfere with it. The desired beauty and order must be achieved, no matter the consequences to be experienced by man since they will not be avoidable, thanks to the human ignorance, limited perceptions, greed and selfishness.

LIFESTYLES

Life is a free gift from The Prime One through the aide of The Great Ones, but it comes with responsibilities which are often mistaken for freedoms by man. It's obvious that we all have our freedoms, but you don't just do what thou wilt just because you assume to be free to doing whatever you assume right to you.

Sometimes assuming so much freedom can be dangerous to an individual's existence and that's the problem with the modern world. When people are allowed to do whatever they please, they oftentimes become reckless. Everything has a limit, and so is freedom, but many are so ignorant to realize this fact. You can live the way you deem appropriate to you, you can do whatever you think is best for you, but how far is so far? How much is too much?

Everyone has their individual freedoms designed by Nature, but responsibility in living has never been understood by man. He is good at identifying all that he can do, but not what he cannot do. He is occupied with how much he has freedom, but not concerned about his responsibility in life. We are always the problem ourselves, but we are so ignorant do accept that fact.

Does it mean that we are the epicenter for existence in this world that if we weren't there everything else would not be there? Does it mean than man is more valuable than anything else that exists? What guarantee is there that you (human), are the prime being in the whole universe, that without you everything else wouldn't be in existence? What makes you think that if you ever gone extinct, someone will mourn the loss?

I've pointed this in a different publication, but I'll repeat again: All must understand that the problems currently experienced in the world, and other crazy experiences to come, are consequences of the human lifestyles. Also note that no one will feel guilty of the consequences which will hit the human race. Destruction is unavoidable and even the life (as perceived by man) will be "put on the line" and there will be no mercy; note that clearly.

The Powers that control the world are ruthless to the ignorant.

I know I sound like someone who is evil or who enjoys evil. I know many will call me a sadist and all sorts of names, but whatever it might be, am just doing "my job." I'm just like anyone else and every consequence that will hit humanity will hit me too. I'm just helping in "turning the stones" since none will be left standing. The time for the truth to be addressed as it has come and each must know where they stand. I'm just one among the many others who are aiding the Plan, but that doesn't make me special.

Man has to change the way he lives his life if he has to see the light of the day once the "sun rises." Certain lifestyles must be shunned if humanity has to survive. The focus on the self only has to be changed and the good of all be the "new normal." As of writing this, there are some things which have happened worldwide and man (if he can really see) has started to realize the fact that no one is special or above what's ahead.

It has been all about individual satisfactions and interests, but when the core of man is touched with the "holly wood" of sympathy, kindness and the like through the happenstances around him, he realizes that even money will never save him, but can be used to help the other person. People now are aware (if they really are), that no matter what you have, it can sometimes become useless if only used as a tool of self benefit only.

Simplicity is the key to human progression.

We have people who depend wholly throughout their lives on luxurious meaningless lifestyles, travels worldwide and the like just for fun, while so many people are dying of hunger, many homeless, and the like. I have no problem with the perceived wealthy that spend their lives using their wealth for their individual fun and the like since that doesn't concern me, but what's the meaning of wealth if you cannot use it on a common good other than the self?

What's the value of having so much wealth, but you do nothing to others, only yourself? Luckily, what's coming doesn't give a damn on who one assumes to be, and neither do I and so won't sugarcoat anything to please men. However I don't want to claim that everyone wealthy is selfish. There are many who have dedicated in helping others, we always see and know and are grateful for these kinds of people since it's these kinds who will bring about the right human relation which we are seeking to impart to humanity.

As of now we can see people starting to have sympathetic hearts and trying to help those who need it, due to circumstances of course. People are starting to realize that in spite of being wealthy, influential, powerful, and the like, those identities and perceptions matter less and so must use what they have to serve a common good.

It's unfortunate that some of these qualities must be learnt the hard way since man has proven to be a "slow-learner." Circumstances however will make him learn quickly and grasp the ideas being passed on and produce ideals which are all-inclusive, rather than the present which has been a part of the modern world which have been all selfish and personal. The hard way has proven to be the only way to the human realization of the universality of Life and existence.

As we move along the path to "human awakening" to reality as it is, many things will happen which will be considered evil, but whatever they will yield in the end will be beneficial to humanity and the world at large. Many people are yet to see what's really happening because of ignorance and wrong perception of things as they are; but those with eyes can start to see some sense of concern to many, on the need to help their fellow kind.

That's the path the world is being led towards, but since what we assume to be reality blinds us from seeing, with ignorance and limited beliefs and perceptions being a part of the "normal life," there is so much we are yet to experience. The darkness that is ahead will open man's eyes and lead him to the realization that without cooperation with his fellow kind, he will go nowhere.

Circumstances will force man to adjust and change his present lifestyles and seek those ways which are incorporating everyone and which are focused on goodwill as the new way of life. It's through this that balance will be attained and labels, social classes and the like will vanish, and people start identifying with the whole, not with the present divisive classes and destructive lifestyles.

LOVE AND HUMAN RELATIONS

Everyone sings of the term love, but not everyone understands the true meaning of it. Sometimes the most obvious things are the hardest to comprehend. Even a small child can give you the meaning of love, and everyone professes it all the time, but is it really love?

We see this claim of love everywhere, in friendships, relationships, marriages, and the like. This term has become so basic that it has lost its meaning. I've mentioned this in a different material, but will just repeat; am not tired of repeating things.

First, whatever people call love isn't. It doesn't matter what you believe in, but that's a fact. Much of the human perceived love revolves around individual interests and emotions. "God is love" right? If then whatever we consider to be love truly is, then it can also mean that relationships are love too, isn't it? Don't be misled by ideologies which have been intended to mislead you and keeping you restrained, since you will forever live in darkness and will never see The Light of the Day.

I know many will start assuming that I'm demeaning relationships but my point is that even if called love, this is a lower aspect which is not truly love as perceived, but rather an emotional expression of an individual towards another. LOVE is not guided by emotion or personal interests, but rather a higher aspect of virtue which is never guided by feelings.

Love has never expressed itself in the world, since it has not yet been released to the world by its Custodian.

The human existence is confined in the lower natures which are only guided and run by emotions, feelings, personal interests, and the like. Through the human focus and concentration on form, everything he does is in line of the same form in that all he does is to satisfy it and meet its desires and needs. By this, everyone assumes that whatever they think as real is truly real, and this becomes part of their perception and understanding.

23

The human existence is cocooned in the lower natures and animal instincts of survival and it's by this that we witness everyone on the run trying to seek to satisfy their desires and needs of the form nature only. With the confusion that has blanketed the world for eons, and which have become a part of human existence, everything is understood basing on the level of perception of an individual and on the manner in which it's mainly applied on personal level.

Man stays like a jungle creature which is always alert on the next step to take to prevent himself from sleeping hungry, even if it'll mean to prey on his fellow kind. It's through this that the world today looks like a competition ground, everyone seeking ways to emerge the first or to acquire more than anyone else. This animal mentalities and interests of the self has resulted in many becoming poor, oppressed, murdered and the like, just to pave way for a few to emerge as "winners" to satisfy their individual urges.

We might claim we have right human relations and love, but the truth is that it's all fantasy. There is no right human relation in the world; there is no love, only people who are just after personal interests and who are seeking individual prosperities just to feel satisfied and accomplished in their own levels of perception.

LOVE will only be available to humanity once they understand the value of existence and know how to relate with each other. Just because you claim to love, that doesn't guarantee that you truly do. Remember that most of what we believe, perceive or understand is only based on our individual interests. For example a non-believer will find the religious materials irrelevant to them, even if it has something beneficial to them as individuals. And as well, the religious fellows will ignore anything else that doesn't support their belief systems (like this material).

We always like what we want, not because it's of value to us, but because it supports our ideologies or mode of reasoning. The same way applies to love and human relations; we can claim that we love each other, we can claim that we are relating rightly with our brothers, but it's only an assumption based on our own perceptions just because we want to justify ourselves.

LOVE has no gender, class, boundary or identity. However, don't use my words to justify the present world's rotten morals from a few misled individuals with their limited perceptions and reasoning (Though that doesn't bother us anyway). My reference is not on the human understanding of love, so let my points be clear. Man has to learn the way to coexist with his fellow kind and incorporate everyone.

Hate has overtaken Love in the world, though disguising itself with the perception that because there is no war, there is love. We are all hypocrites in one way or another, and that's why you can laugh with someone, refer to them as your friend and the like, but in the next minute, they will be plotting your demise. Humans have always been taking things and even existence in face-value and that's why even our interrelations with each other are hypocritical and illusory.

Darkness overshadows the light in the present world, but with the artificial lights from individual creations, everyone assumes they are living in the light of day. We perceive everything the way we want, and that's why so much is still hidden to humanity due to the limited perceptions and concentration on form and being blinded by glamour.

A time is coming when so much crazy stuff will be faced globally, and people will realize that they have been living lies. A time when each will discover that they have been lying to themselves and everything that they have been valuing was not even important at all. It's at that time that people will start feeling the urgency of something beyond their limited interests and perceptions and that's when they will start to seek right human relations which are not only concerned with form, but rather those which serve something superior.

Perfection in existence exists, but it's always hard to be achieved by man due to his perceptions and wrong applications of ideas "handed down" to him. It's funny that even what I share will always be interpreted differently by different people depending on their individual interests and perceptions, though that won't change their intended meanings anyway.

The same applies to everything that man does and perceives since he first serves his desires and interests, which makes it hard for him to discover more than his superficial understanding. We have huge problems at hand which we have to first solve before the "door" can be opened. It's very funny how humans take up things and interpret the way they assume to be the meaning then start doing with the perception of being "cool" without even any clue of what they are doing.

We see this all over and in every human level and it's the same when it comes to human relations and perception of love. The human mind is easily aroused by new things, but it never takes time to dig deeper into the intended meanings and applications. The "Ruthless World Teacher" is just monitoring the world class, waiting for the time to start teaching his lessons, and LOVE is the first subject that humanity must learn. Please note my selection of words in my works when talking about certain subjects since they will give the seriousness of the matter at hand.

Hate must be wiped out in the world and LOVE to take over. Humans must change their perceptions about love and start having the right relations with each other. Integrity must guide the human existence. Man has to learn the right human virtues which are beyond his perceptions, personal interests, desires and the like, and it's through this that Order will be established and the New World will be born.

THE TAKE-OVER

I know now what runs through the minds of many when they read the sub-topic; don't let my words confuse you. I don't mean that the world will be taken over by anyone, but with what is ahead, there are some things that man should know and be aware of. Always know that everything is always in good hands, and no matter how things might seem from the eye view, there is always so much happening that is never visible but which helps in the creation of the visible.

With the present world problems and what is still on the way, many will lose hope, fear and feel desperate in that they will have nowhere to run to or no one to cry to. Many worldwide will feel alone and even wish they were dead due to the ugly ordeal which humanity will face. Like I mentioned in a different material, even a god or whatever one believes in will be nowhere to help those who believe in it.

Man will try to seek help from the things he valued but even at that time those things will be nowhere to be found. He will feel lost and alone, and it's unfortunate that at that time the animal instincts of survival will be expressed hugely with each person seeking to save their individual lives. Before man awakens to unity, the survival mentalities will be so potent that even someone would kill his brother for food.

Things will turn so ugly that the world will be filled with darkness (literally) that man will feel like the end has finally come and feel like he has been abandoned by his Creator. However, all the global happenstances will be just lessons that man must learn and understand to give him the pass to The New Day with the right mindset.

There is something I must say which man has to understand. Despite the craziness in the world, it doesn't mean that man is alone. Yes he might seem alone, but what if I told you that there are certain Beings Who are among men as we speak and who are on a "Special Mission" in the world? What if I told you that maybe you've even come across one or several of them, only that you didn't know since they look just like you and were born just like any other human being?

I know how crazy this looks and might not make sense to many (I've mentioned this in my first book). The Powers that control the world are after something and are serving a certain Plan and through this, they have to establish certain points in the world where this Plan will be carried forth, and through this They send certain Masters to be among men and help in the execution of this Plan.

Like I mentioned in the first material, these Masters among men will never be known, but walk among us. They walk among us, fight the daily battles of life like any other person, and interestingly, some might not even be aware that they are Masters. Some of these Beings operate as channels through which the energies of change are operated through in the world. They act as centers of dispersal. I don't mean that they are activists, and for your information, they might even not be playing any role in the public arena since their time is yet.

They are the "magnets" and transformers of the world and soon (some may have already started) they will start their work (whether in the shadows or publicly). Some might be aware of their duties as of now, while others might not be yet aware of who they really are, and some might be perfecting and mastering their craft and collecting their "tools of work" together in preparation for the Great Work ahead of helping The Hierarchy and all The Great Ones in executing the Plan.

If need will permit, humanity will know them, though they might remain mysteries and unknown since their work is not self-service, and so will seek no personal recognition. When the time is right, they will take over and start their individual tasks of which they might not generally work them alone. Some might collect their individual followers and teach them so as to take their tasks forth.

There is no guarantee that humanity will know these Beings or even notice their duties and impacts to the world and so much might still remain like a theory. However, it must be understood that the impacts of these Beings is so big that they will change the world and give man the right perspectives of life and help in liberating man from his restraints.

As of now, all of these Masters are among us, learning man and his ways of life and how to approach his problems and on how to help him discover more than he thinks he know. But still, their helpers are still "coming" so as to help them in their duties once their time has come. Due to the emergency that is at the horizons, there are a huge number of helpers who are coming to add force to the duties of these Masters.

I know this will not make sense to many and might even never make sense, but be aware that although we might seem same, we might not generally be. There are various beings who walk among us, who were born like any other human, who look just like any other human, who are struggling in life like any other human and the like, but who "carry the burden of humanity on their backs." However, this doesn't mean that they are special or more important than any other since they face every challenge faced by each one of us; even to some extent they face harder challenges than the rest.

We will never know who they really are, but they are here. We walk our streets with them, they are just waiting for the green light and they take up their duties and bring about order in a chaotic world which we reside in. They are like the "saviors" of humanity in the hour of need. They are here for something greater than themselves and so might never be in the limelight the whole of their lives.

Are you among them? Time will tell.

Please note that I didn't say that I was one of Them and so don't want to create a wrong perception of myself. I'm just sharing what the world needs to know because the time has come for it to be known.

UNITY OF THE TWO

We all have certain perspectives on life and about life basing it on our own interests where we value whatever suits us and disregard whatever that doesn't favor our desires. It's through this that we have what is commonly called individual "tastes" on things or people.

As human beings, we have things that we value and others that we don't, whether ignoring them or just never noticing that they exist. The human life is mostly focused on one side of life while the other remains dormant and unrealized. Both the physical and the invisible are very important to the human existence; with the physical producing the medium of expression and the invisible producing Life itself.

However, we only focus on the medium, assuming it to be the life that we live. Yes we live as physical beings, but the physical expression is useless if life isn't present. Ninety per cent of our lives are focused on form, while the ten per cent remaining is shared among irrelevant things which are illusory like belief systems and the like.

There is no balance in life and that's why there is so much confusion in the world. Much of our lives are just on burdens which are not important, only retarding our growth and slowing down our development. For example everyone is in search of money and wealth that we even forget why we exist. We are so consumed in searching, that we even forget what we already have within us.

Yes wealth is important, but what if you had everything material but empty inside? If we can balance our search for wealth with the search of our divinity, I think there could be so much achievement in the world. By the search of divinity I don't suggest the following of a dogmatic religious or cultural belief; as of now you are aware that I value less the two since they have proven less valuable to the human existence.

Like I previously stated, no one can help you in connecting with your higher self, only yourself alone since that's a personal journey. If the search of wealth takes a fifty per cent, then the search of our divinity should take the rest fifty per cent. It's through balancing the two that so much will be achieved and everything that we seek become not only beneficial to one individual, but many others. This will be attained since the wealth we seek will be used to serve others as well.

The problem with the human existence is that we take so much time on form that we forget that we are not here to serve it, but to use it to serve something greater than it. The form cannot exist without life, though life can exist without form; note that and be aware that as a human being, you have the duty to balance the two and ensure that form serves life, not life serving form. This includes serving others as well, since it's paramount in the world.

The world is chaotic and confused due to the fact that even our individual lives are unbalanced for being self-centered. We seek financial freedom, but only end up becoming slaves to it rather than attaining the freedom that we sought. I've witnessed wealthy people, with millions in almost ten bank accounts, but they live a stressful life. A life which looks great from the outside, but once you listen and watch them closely, they are never happy and don't even enjoy their wealth; you even wonder what's the point of having it if it'll never make you happy.

I don't write theories, speculations or conspiracies. Everything is based on experience and personal witnessing of these things in man. I've seen people even deny themselves some things, just because they are aware that in the process of solving their individual problems, someone else might also benefit in the process. They have money, and everyday money is coming in, but since they don't want to use it on anything that is beneficial to anyone else apart from themselves, they never enjoy it.

For example, a person will be wealthy, have millions in the bank, but uses tap water which is distributed by local authorities. Whenever there is shortage, or rationing, they are suffering just like any other person, yet they are living in their own land, not renting. The reason is that all the neighbors are all dependent on tap water, and if he/she would drill a borehole in his/her compound, the neighbors will be dependent on its water whenever there is a rationing. I don't want to give advice on how one should use their money, and neither am I a financial adviser but these things happen. People deny themselves things, just to prevent someone else from benefiting in the process and in the process live worthless lives. The example is a true story.

Wealth is very important, but are you using it for something important as well apart from your own joys? Or are you among those who claim that their money is only theirs since no one helped them attain it? I've lived with these kinds of people, worked with them and worked for them. We are here to serve, that's basic to existence, and it's only through this service to others that so much will be attained; both individually and globally by humanity.

If you have wealth, use it to transform the lives of others in the way you deem fit to you. If you are an expert in a certain area (whether academic or general), use it to help others as well. Each has something to offer others in their own unique way, the same this guy EM KHEI is using these materials to serve something higher than himself and in leading humanity to the realization of some things which are beneficial to man's existence.

Seek, but use that which you attain to serve.

It all depends on how one chooses to use what they have to serve not himself, but others. When we balance this, the world will enjoy the fruits which will be borne from these individual acts and right human relations will emerge and unity in diversity established worldwide. Through this, Love will be released among men and harmony will rule the world.

If we could focus on balancing our individual lives; seeking to balance form and life, and seeking to serve other than being selfish with what we have (wealth or talent), so much will be attained and each individual's spark will eventually light up the world and order will rule humanity, and the chaos which has been a part of the old world will vanish and the New World will be born where love is supreme and harmony a part of daily life.

CONCLUSION

I know I didn't cover everything in this material, but I hope that whatever I've covered is of importance and will shed a light to the reader. I cannot be in a position of sharing everything, but the most important things which can even be used to discover the other areas of value have been outlined.

All should understand that the desired beauty will eventually be revealed and man live as per the Plan. The time for the old ways is ending, and man has to adapt to change and live in accordance with what is desired. However, he has to start his work on himself before extending it to his fellow kind. He has to discover the chaos in his personal life and seek order, rising above monotonies, beliefs and mentalities which are useless to his existence and seek something greater than himself.

The global chaos present now all generate from individuals then extend to the world, which means that the solution shall therefore come from individuals. Each must start to work on themselves, shun little mentalities and perceptions, selfishness and the like. Man must learn service and seek beyond his limited reality, for it is only then that he will find peace in his individual life and that will in time result to the global harmony and order will be evident in the world.

Words say that history repeats itself, not in everything though, but for ages, humanity has been learning important lessons the hard way. Humans prove to be incapable of learning on their own, with the "little things" never making sense to them and always seeking to see proof of everything for it to make sense to them.

Radical changes are expected in the world and for your information, this will not require public opinion, votes or political representation to be discussed of whether they are worthy or not. The changes needed in the world will be enacted and order must be established, whether seen as "evil" by man or not, that won't change a thing. Man therefore has a duty of changing his ways, mode of thinking, beliefs, lifestyles, and the like if he wants to see the light of The New Day.

The world must be rearranged and the human life must as well be transformed from superficial concentration, to higher ideals. Man must learn responsibility and live responsibly in all his endeavors. A cancer patient is faced by death when they are not willing to sacrifice their ailing part. The patient must be ready for the removal of the tumor, and continue with treatment to ensure that all of their body isn't affected by the disease. Even if it means to remove a leg, hand and the like, where the disease has accumulated itself, the patient must be ready to do it for the good of their overall health.

The same applies to humanity. Man must be willing to sacrifice his limited mentalities, beliefs, useless and unhealthy lifestyles, and the like for his survival. He must be ready to change for better and shun his lower natures for higher aspects which guide Life and existence. Man must live in accordance with the Plan and strive for using his existence for the benefit of others.

Remember, if humanity becomes a cancer to the world, they will be removed for the benefit of the other kingdoms in nature and no one will regret it (I've emphasized that in a different material). Man should understand that he is not the center of the Universe and so he can be wiped off the earth even without a second thought if he proves poison to it.

Everyone has a duty; everyone has a responsibility in their own level to seek beyond the illusory reality that we exist in. Nothing is wrong with the world, and nothing is wrong with the things that are there, but what is wrong is the way humans use them.

If we want to change the world for better we have to change ourselves first. Everything must change, or the world is faced with a very huge mess. Lifestyles must change and new ones emerge which are not selfish and poisonous. Hate must be shun and right human relationships which are sincere and honest be established among men. Ignorance must be treaded on and replaced by responsibility, participation and the quest of the truth. Useless beliefs which are just after separation and hypocrisy must end and replaced with individual illumination. Useless officials and petty laws which serve no good must be replaced with true leaders and laws which seek the betterment of those ruled.

The darkness and chaos that fills the earth must be replaced by the light of The New Day and order be established. Man has to seek higher ideals, seeking to use his life on things of value not only to himself but to others as well. Service must be the "new normal" and so much will be attained in the world and so much will be revealed to man and he will awaken to reality as it is. After order is attained, humanity will live as a family, free of limited identities and perceptions, each striving for a common good and LOVE will pour in the world.

Everyone is a player, and everyone has a part on the great task of transformation. How will you use your existence for the benefit of not only yourself? How is your individual life going to change for better? How will you incorporate everyone in your endeavors? How will you play your part?

Let your life never be wasted in form and on useless things. Find a way to solve your individual problems and differences which you perceive to have from the others. Use your life on something greater than yourself, serve your brothers and seek to unify, not divide. Every individual effort has a very big impact, though not realized by man; it can shape the humanity's future or destroy it.

THREE THIRTEEN.

Printed in Great Britain
by Amazon

10262839R00031